DOOMSDAY ROCKS FROM SPACE

Bizarre Science

Margaret Poynter

Enslow Publishers, Inc.
40 Industrial Road
Box 398
Berkeley Heights, NJ 07922
USA

http://www.enslow.com

Original edition published as *Killer Asteroids* in 1996.

Library of Congress Cataloging-in-Publication Data

Poynter, Margaret.
  [Killer asteroids]
  Doomsday rocks from space / Margaret Poynter.
     p. cm. — (Bizarre science)
  Summary: "Discusses comets, asteroids, and meteors, including how and where they are formed in space, what scientists are doing to study and track them, and what danger these doomsday rocks are to Earth"—Provided by publisher.
  Previously published as: Killer asteroids.
  Includes bibliographical references and index.
  ISBN 978-0-7660-3673-4
  1. Asteroids—Orbits—Juvenile literature. 2. Catastrophes (Geology)—Juvenile literature. I. Title.
  QB377.P69 2011
  523.44—dc22
                          2009053601

Paperback ISBN 978-1-59845-221-1

Printed in the United States of America

092010 Lake Book Manufacturing, Inc., Melrose Park, IL

10 9 8 7 6 5 4 3 2 1

To Our Readers:
We have done our best to make sure all Internet addresses in this book were active and appropriate when we went to press. However, the author and the publisher have no control over and assume no liability for the material available on those Internet sites or on other Web sites they may link to. Any comments or suggestions can be sent by e-mail to comments@enslow.com or to the address on the back cover.

♻ Enslow Publishers, Inc., is committed to printing our books on recycled paper. The paper in every book contains 10% to 30% post-consumer waste (PCW). The cover board on the outside of each book contains 100% PCW. Our goal is to do our part to help young people and the environment too.

Illustration Credits: Courtesy of Bob Walters and Laura Fields, p. 7; Photo by Brett Simison / Institute for Astronomy, University of Hawaii, p. 37; Carl Goodman / Photo Researchers, Inc., p. 40; Chris Butler / Photo Researchers, Inc., p. 24; D. McDavid (Limber Observatory), D.C. Boice (SwRI), p. 30; David A. Hardy / Photo Researchers, Inc., p. 1; Detlev van Ravenswaay / Photo Researchers, Inc., pp. 26, 34, 36; Don Davis / NASA, p. 9; Joe Tucciarone / Photo Researchers, Inc., p. 12; Ken Lucas / Visuals Unlimited, Inc., p. 10; NASA, pp. 17, 38; NASA, ESA, and H. Hammel (Space Science Institute), p. 43; NASA, ESA, and H. Weaver and E. Smith (STScl), p. 42; NASA / JPL, pp. 18, 22; NASA / JPL-Caltech, p. 28; NASA / JPL / Space Science Institute, p. 32; NASA / McREL, p. 21; Richard Bizley / Photo Researchers, Inc., p. 4; © Shutterstock®, p. 15.

Cover Illustration: David A. Hardy / Photo Researchers, Inc. (Illustration of a large asteroid colliding with Earth on the Yucatán Peninsula in Mexico 65 million years ago).

CONTENTS

The Reign of the Dinosaur

They were here long before human beings existed. Some of them lived in hilly areas. Others thundered across the low plains. A few made their homes in dry deserts. Many more lived in lush forests. Still, others spent their lives sloshing through swamps and large ponds. These largest and strongest of the world's creatures were found everywhere. For 140 million years, they ruled Earth.

They are now called dinosaurs, the "terrible lizards," though they were not lizards. Many of these reptiles were peaceful and harmless, not terrible. These creatures shared their world with other types of reptiles, and with insects, frogs, turtles, snails, and small mammals.

A doomsday rock on its speedy path toward Earth's atmosphere.

Dinosaurs came in many different shapes and sizes. Some walked on all fours. Some were so heavy that they lived in swamps where the water could support their bodies. Still, others stood on their hind legs, balanced by their tails.

There were dinosaurs that were only two feet long. One of the largest may have been 125 feet (38 meters) long. Some were as tall as a six-story building. It is believed that the heaviest dinosaur weighed more than fifty tons.[1]

Not all dinosaurs were carnivores—that is, meat-eaters. Many of them were herbivores; they survived on diets of leaves and grass. The larger plant-eaters had to eat a ton of leaves a day to stay alive.

It used to be thought that all dinosaurs were cold-blooded creatures. They needed the sun to warm them up; otherwise, they were sluggish and slow moving, like reptiles and amphibians today. Now it is thought that at least some of the dinosaurs were warm-blooded.[2] Like human beings, they produced their own heat when their muscles burned the food they ate. Such creatures could have been able to move as quickly as cats.

A Different World

The world of the dinosaurs was very different from the world of today. There were reptiles everywhere—on the land, in lakes, in the sea, and in the air. There were few hot or cold areas. In most places, the climate was warm and balmy.

Dinosaurs ruled the earth for millions of years.

At the beginning of the dinosaurs' reign, all the earth's land was lumped together in one mass, dotted with small inland seas. There were no great oceans to interrupt the animals' movements and no towering mountain ranges to block their paths.

The earth's surface is made up of interlocking plates, which are sections of land. These plates are always on the move. Because of this movement, the single landmass began to break up 150 million years ago. Huge chunks of land drifted away. Those pieces became the seven continents. Great mountain ranges rose when continents collided. The inland seas drained into the ocean. In some places, the mild climate became cold. In others, it became much warmer. The average temperature rose by as much as twenty degrees. Some of the smaller creatures escaped the heat by creeping under brush and twigs. Others burrowed under clumps of weeds and grass.

Over long periods of time, millions of years, some places got drier or wetter, colder or hotter. Dinosaurs and other animals moved to different places. In the hot areas, the dinosaurs could not cool off. They had no sweat glands to release their body heat. When they panted, their mouths dried out. Those that were in dry areas dragged their great weight to the nearest water hole. As time passed, some dinosaurs died from the heat and lack of water.

Most dinosaurs, however, evolved with their new environments. Their senses were keen, they were alert and aggressive, and they were very adaptable. The world was changing, but the dinosaurs still ruled that world.

The Endless Night

Then, about 65 million years ago, catastrophe struck. In one area, there was a huge explosion—an unknown object had smashed into Earth. Dinosaurs grazing nearby were killed instantly. The impact of the explosion was probably felt hundreds of miles away. The initial heat blast may have killed many dinosaurs. Then, tons of dust, ash, and soot filled the atmosphere. For months, the heat and light of the sun could not penetrate this dust cloud. The skies were dark, and the earth grew colder and colder. There were snowstorms.

Flying dinosaurs soar above the clouds as a giant object crashes into Earth. This catastrophe most likely caused the dinosaurs' extinction.

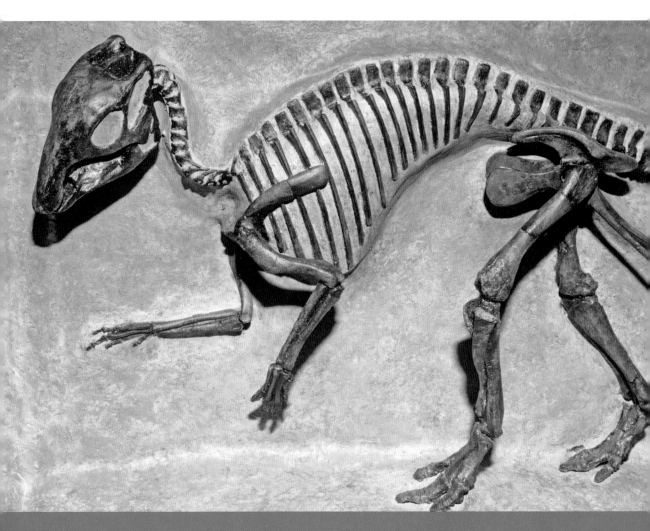

A dinosaur skeleton found in the United States. The course of evolution changed after the dinosaurs became extinct.

Blundering about in the darkness, the remaining herbivores stripped the trees of every last leaf. Some of the hardier ones survived for a time by digging through the snow for grass and moss. They ate twigs and chewed the bark off dead trees. Eventually, even that food supply was gone.

The surviving carnivores continued to feast on their starving plant-eating cousins and other mammals. When there was no more prey, the ravenous creatures turned on each other.

As time passed, the dust cloud began to disappear. Within ten years, it was gone. This caused sweltering temperatures. After this, the dinosaurs became extinct. So had at least two thirds of the other species of plants and animals living on Earth. The course of evolution had been changed forever.

What caused the sudden, drastic events that led to the destruction of the dinosaurs? Could such a disaster ever occur again? To find the answers to those questions, scientists have looked for clues on Earth.

They have also looked at outer space. Is there something out there that could destroy us as it destroyed the dinosaurs?

Many experts believe the answer to that question is "Yes."[3]

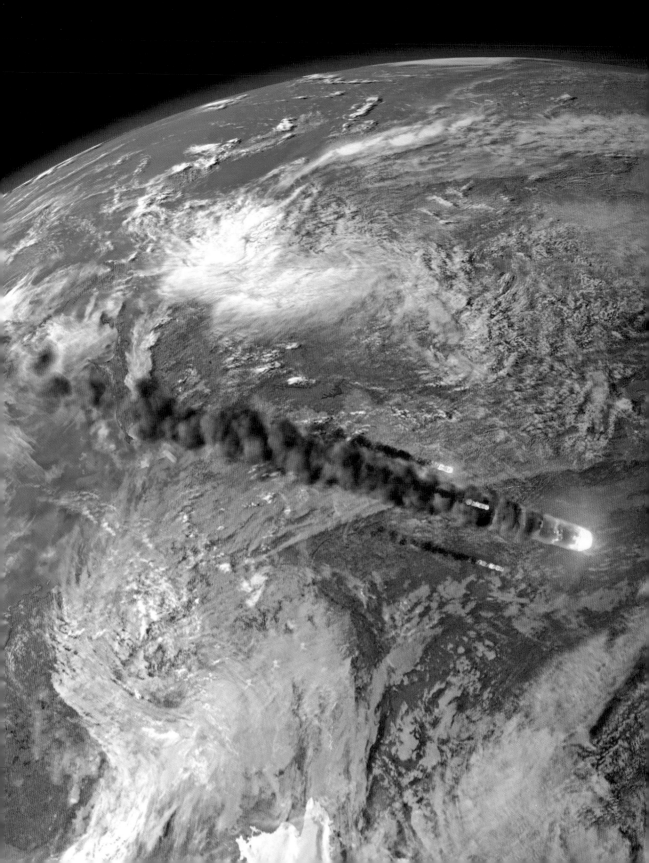

The Search for Clues

It was the morning of June 30, 1908. The Trans-Siberian Express was making its regular run across the plains of northern Russia. Its conductor was startled when he heard a series of loud bangs. *Has there been an accident?* he wondered.[1] After stopping the train, he rushed back to the passenger car. There, a group of wide-eyed men and women said that they had heard the same noises—what sounded like explosions. Looking out the windows toward the source of the sounds, they had seen a bright blue ball of flame streaking across the sky. It had left a trail of smoke behind it.

Residents of the sparsely populated area had also seen and heard the explosion. Some of them lived near the 830 square

An illustration shows the Tunguska meteorite approaching Siberia, Russia, in 1908. The meteorite produced a huge fireball after exploding in Earth's atmosphere.

miles (2,150 square kilometers) of forest that had been uprooted by the shock waves. Thirty miles (forty-eight kilometers) away, others saw the bodies of the reindeer that had been killed by the blast. The tents of nomads camping several miles away were scattered. The clothes of a man who had been standing sixty miles (ninety-seven kilometers) away caught on fire.

Because Russia was involved in wars and revolutions at this time, it was not until 1927 that scientists could safely travel to Siberia. There, they found the remains of the fallen forest. They saw small remnants of an object scattered over a wide area. There were also a number of small holes these remnants had made when they had landed.

Many people have since tried to explain the mysterious event. Some say that an alien spaceship had exploded. Others say that a black hole had been bored into Earth and had come out in the Atlantic Ocean. Most experts have a more reasonable answer. They believe that a giant meteorite, a piece of rocky or metallic space debris, had crashed onto Earth's surface.[2]

Known as the Tunguska event, scientists now know that the blast did not occur on Earth's surface. It had taken place five miles up in our atmosphere producing a fireball and a cloud of dust and tiny fragments. It is estimated that the explosion had the force of 12 million tons of TNT, a powerful explosive. It was eight hundred times more powerful than the force of the atomic bomb that leveled Hiroshima in 1945.

Bombardment from Space

Space debris has been falling on Earth for billions of years. It will continue falling as long as Earth exists. Each day, three or four twenty-pound (nine-kilogram) meteorites strike Earth's surface. Once every hundred years, a 4,000-ton meteorite falls from the sky, and once every 100,000 years, a meteorite weighing 50,000 tons or more plows into our small planet.

Earth's surface is scarred by at least one hundred craters that resulted from collisions with large space objects. Only 50,000 years ago, a 150-foot-wide (46-meter) nickel-iron meteorite smashed into what is now northern Arizona. At impact, it was

The 150-foot-wide meteorite that smashed into northern Arizona 50,000 years ago created this giant crater.

traveling about twenty-five thousand miles (forty thousand kilometers) per hour. The force of the collision sent 300 million tons of rock flying high into the air. It left a vast crater 660 feet deep (201 meters) and about four thousand feet (twelve hundred meters) wide. That crater could swallow a sixty-story building or hold eleven football fields.

Such a large object causes a lot of damage to the environment. Could a meteorite have led to the extinction of the dinosaurs? For many years, scientists tried to answer that question. In the late 1970s, Walter Alvarez, a geologist, was in Italy. He was studying a thin layer of clay that lay between two layers of rock. This same layer of clay exists in various parts of the world. The rock above the clay had been formed later than the rock below it. The clay marked the boundary between two geologic eras. A geologic era is a period of time in history. Each era is marked by distinctive types of rock and rock formations.

As Alvarez poked and pried into the bottom layer of rock, he found dinosaur fossils embedded in it. He then examined the upper layer of rock. In that layer, there were no such fossils. That layer of clay must have been formed at the same time that the dinosaurs vanished.

Later, other scientists studied samples of the same clay. One of them was Walter's father, Luis, a physicist. The team made an important and exciting discovery: There were traces of iridium in the clay. Iridium is a metal that is seldom found naturally on Earth's surface. It is, however, often found in meteorites.

A Doomsday Rock

Other geologic studies found iridium in the same layer of clay in other parts of the world. There were also bits of glassy rock called tektites, which are formed when asteroid debris mixes with superhot gases. These and other discoveries led to a startling conclusion: 65 million years ago, a giant asteroid 6.2 miles (9.9 kilometers) wide must have slammed into Earth. When the huge, fast-moving object plowed into the ground, there was a rapid release of energy.

A NASA scientist collects soil samples at the edge of the Meteor Crater in Arizona. Scientists study the craters left by meteorites to learn about when the object landed on Earth.

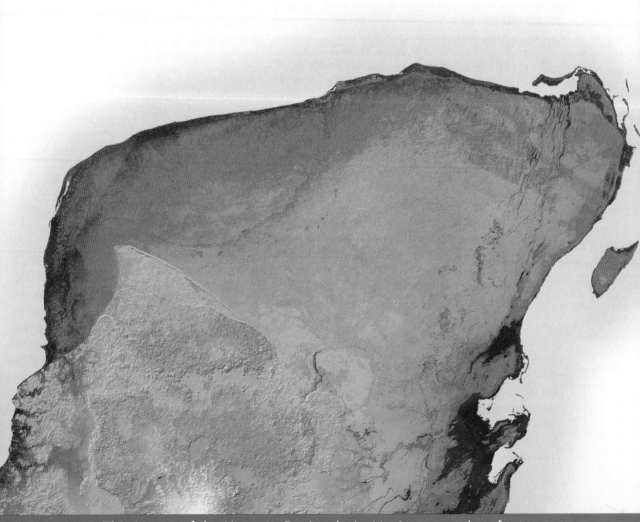

This image of the Yucatán Peninsula in Mexico was taken from a spacecraft. The image shows part of the impact crater from the asteroid that crashed into Earth 65 million years ago. The crater in the surface looks like a semicircle in the upper left corner of the peninsula.

That energy was converted into heat. Most of the asteroid vaporized; it changed into gas. The rocks close by the crash scene were also vaporized. The vapor expanded and exploded. The blast was ten thousand times more powerful than the combined explosions of all the nuclear weapons in the world today. It left a deep crater in the ground. The dust and debris from the crater were thrown high into the atmosphere.

Does the crater caused by this doomsday rock still exist? Had it survived the eroding forces of wind and rain? Many experts believe they know the exact spot where the asteroid crashed to Earth.[3] This spot is in what is now Mexico's Yucatán Peninsula. There, a mile underground, is a circular crater 190 miles (306 kilometers) wide. Scientific testing of rock samples taken from the rim of this mammoth hole shows that this rock was once melted, and then it hardened. These samples resembled volcanic rock, but the rock had not melted slowly, as volcanic rock does. These rocks had melted suddenly, as they would in an explosion.

Studies showed that this melted rock was formed 65 million years ago, when the layer of clay was formed. It was at this same time that the dinosaurs disappeared from Earth.

Life in the Fast Lane

We still do not know the entire truth about why the dinosaurs disappeared. We do know that, at various times, other species have suddenly vanished. Some of those cases have also been linked to objects from space colliding with our planet.

It is not surprising that these collisions occur, because Earth is like a spaceship. Traveling 65,000 miles (105,000 kilometers) per hour, it makes continuous voyages around the sun. Earth is not alone in its travels: Like a freeway during rush hour or a school hallway between class periods, the space in our solar system contains a lot of traffic. Whizzing past Earth in the same or the opposite direction, there are specks of dust and grains of sand, pebbles, small rocks, and boulders as large as trucks or houses.

Asteroids

In space, there are also huge chunks of stone or metal; some are the size of mountains, others the size of small cities. The largest of these "flying mountains" is 600 miles (nearly 1,000 kilometers) in diameter. These miniature planets have craters from past impacts with other large objects.

In this artist's illustration, a spacecraft gathers data from an asteroid.

Through a telescope, these larger pieces of space rubble look like points of light. The ancient Greeks thought they were stars. Today, we call them asteroids, which is Greek for "starlike." Asteroids are leftovers from the creation of our solar system 4.5 billion years ago. Some are pieces that were chipped off another asteroid during a collision. Some asteroids are made of rock and

Jupiter

Mar

The asteroid belt lies between Mars and Jupiter, as shown here in a diagram of the solar system.

others have cores of dense metal. Some have smaller asteroids orbiting around them.

The asteroid belt lies between Mars and Jupiter, where there is plenty of room. Their orbits may remain stable for millions of years. Sometimes, however, two asteroids collide. In this game of cosmic billiards, one of them gets knocked out of its orbit. Eventually, it is caught by the gravity of a larger body. It may keep traveling in a shortened orbit, or it may collide with the larger body. Most of the craters on the moons and planets of our solar system are the result of collisions with asteroids.

Earth's gravity pulls a few asteroids into our planet's neighborhood. Currently, there are more than a hundred known asteroids whose orbits cross Earth's orbit. An asteroid travels at ten to thirty miles (sixteen to forty-eight kilometers) a second. When a building-sized asteroid smacks into our atmosphere, friction heats it up to thousands of degrees. When it gets hot enough, it blows up with a blinding flash of light called a meteor.

From Earth, these meteors, or shooting stars, appear to be streaks of light across the night sky. The smaller meteors go *pffft* and disappear from view in the blink of an eye. The larger ones look like bright fireballs. The remnants leave a blazing trail across the sky.

Mammoth fireballs can be created when asteroids explode. At such times, powerful shock waves ripple through Earth's atmosphere. One such event took place high above Indonesia in 1988. The force of the explosion was calculated to be equal to

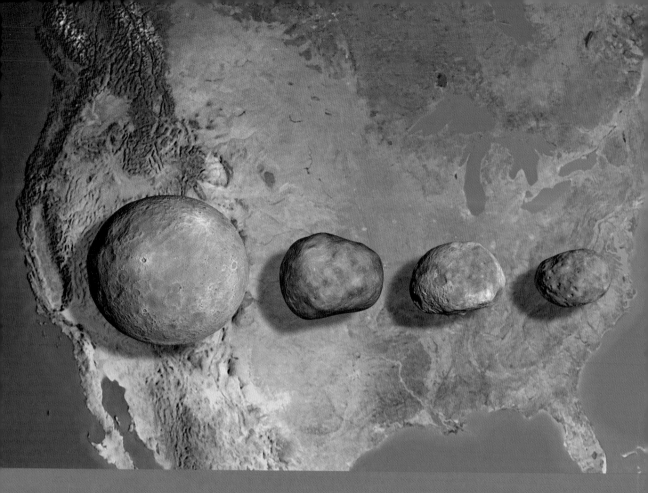

Asteroids come in many sizes. This computer scale artwork shows four asteroids currently in the asteroid belt orbiting in space between Mars and Jupiter. They are seen against North America to show their massive size.

that of five thousand tons of high explosives. Seen from Earth, the meteor looked like a flash of light as bright as the sun.

On February 1, 1994, what may have been a 14 to 44-foot- (4.3 to 13.4-meter-) wide rocky asteroid exploded over the South Pacific. The force of the blast was equal to thousands of tons of TNT. The explosion lit up the sky.

Comets

Astronomers classify comets according to how long they take to orbit the sun. Short-period comets, which come from the Kuiper belt beyond the orbit of Pluto, need less than two hundred years to complete one orbit. Long-period comets take two hundred years or longer. Long-period comets begin in a region even farther (maybe a thousand times farther) beyond Pluto's orbit called the Oort cloud.

At first, comets look like tumbling dirty snowballs. The core is less than ten miles (sixteen kilometers) across. At this stage, they are too far away to be seen from Earth.

Occasionally, a group of young comets is snared by the gravity from a passing star. The comets then travel in an orbit that plunges them from their birthplace toward the sun. During this journey, they pass by Jupiter or Saturn. The paths of some of the comets are changed by the gravity of these planets.

About once every century, a comet careens toward the inner solar system. Somewhere between Jupiter and Mars, the sun's heat turns the comet's frozen gases into vapor. The vapor, combined with particles of ice, streams out behind the comet's core, forming a dust tail.

The core of the comet erupts with great puffs of gas and dust. Like the thrusters on a spacecraft, these puffs cause a very slow change in the comet's orbit. The comet may enter our inner solar system because of its original orbit or the gravitational pull of other planets.

The surface of a comet is shown in this illustration as it approaches Earth's atmosphere. Vapors are rising from the comet because of heat from the sun.

Only a few such stragglers are ever seen from Earth. By that time, they are very old comets. The warmth of the sun is causing them to come apart. Eventually, all the ice melts. All that remains are the rock and dust that form the core. The comet then resembles an asteroid.

An entire comet can fill a space much larger than Earth. The cloud of gas and dust that surrounds the comet's core can be larger than the Sun. Despite its size, a comet has very little mass. This lack of mass means that it does not exert much gravitational pull. It passes closely to moons and planets without disturbing them at all.

On the other hand, a comet can easily be pulled off course by a giant planet—Jupiter, Saturn, or Uranus. It then becomes locked into a shorter orbit and approaches the sun at regular intervals. With each approach, the sun's heat causes more of the comet's ice to melt. The more ice that melts, the shorter the comet's life span becomes.

About two hundred of these periodic comets visit Earth's cosmic neighborhood regularly. The most famous is Halley's Comet, which reappears every seventy-six to seventy-nine years. In 1910, astronomers predicted that Earth would pass through Halley's tail. Some scientists said that we would be exposed to toxic space gases. There was worldwide panic; people pushed and shoved to buy gas masks. Fortunately, the scientists were proved to be wrong.

Another periodic comet is called Swift-Tuttle. It was seen in 1862, then again spotted in September 1992. On November 7, 1992, it passed within 110 million miles (177 million kilometers) of Earth. Each August, Earth crosses Swift-Tuttle's orbit. Even though the comet itself is far away on its 130-year journey around the sun, the particles it left behind remain in orbit. When Earth crosses the orbit, the particles burn up in the atmosphere. From the ground, the burning particles appear to be streaks of light.

A telescope captured this photograph of Halley's Comet on December 13, 1985.

This event is called the Perseid meteor shower. It is one of the most spectacular annual meteor showers.

It has been predicted that Swift-Tuttle will return to Earth's area of space on August 14, 2126. On that date, it will come much closer to our planet than it did in 1992. One astronomer figured it may come within 14 million miles (23 million kilometers) of Earth.[1] It will be moving at 130,000 miles (209,170 kilometers) per hour. There is no doubt that Swift-Tuttle's 2126 meteor shower will be one of the great sky shows of all time.

Outwitting a Doomsday Rock

Swift-Tuttle's core is about five miles (eight kilometers) across. The dinosaurs' doomsday rock was probably close to that size. What if Swift-Tuttle changes its course ever so slightly? What if its jets nudge it toward Earth during its next visit?

For a while, astronomers thought that Earth might be in danger in 2126. Now they believe that Swift-Tuttle will not be a real threat until 3044.[1] If it strikes the earth's surface, so much dust will be thrown into our atmosphere that all crops will die. Many of the world's animals will perish. Very few human beings will survive. The survivors may have to live as our cave-dwelling ancestors lived. They will have to pick berries and dig roots. With luck, they will find a pig or a cow to eat.

Swift-Tuttle could become Earth's doomsday rock; so could at least one hundred other asteroids whose orbits now cross that of our planet. On the average, an object two-thirds of a mile (one

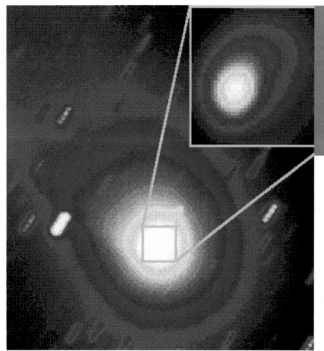

This image shows the Swift-Tuttle Comet, the largest object known to make periodic passes near Earth. Inset is the core, which is about five miles across.

kilometer) wide will strike Earth once every one million years. An object 1.2 miles (two kilometers) wide will strike our planet once every few million years.

Our moon bears the scars of such collisions; so do the other planets and their moons. On Earth, however, it appears that those space objects did more than leave scars. It may have been a visiting comet that furnished the molecules needed for life to develop.[2] Our oceans may have been produced in part by a watery invader from outer space.

What about the dinosaurs' doomsday rock? Before it struck, many primitive mammals fell prey to giant predators. The extinction of the dinosaurs cleared the way for the mammals to thrive and develop, eventually leading to the appearance of the first human beings.

If those humans had been forced to share their planet with giant meat-eating reptiles, they would not have survived. The dinosaurs would still be ruling the earth.

Preventing the Final Disaster

Today, it is unlikely that any good would come to humans if a large comet or asteroid struck Earth. So far, such an object has not landed in a highly populated area, but what if the object that exploded over Siberia in 1908 had slammed into a large city? It could have destroyed hundreds of buildings. It could have killed tens of thousands of people.

Experts agree that sometime in the future, such an object could cause either a local or a worldwide catastrophe.[3] If nothing is done, human beings might go the way of the dinosaurs. The difference is that prehistoric creatures could not save themselves. They did not even know they were in danger.

Because of modern scientific knowledge, we are now aware of the danger. The challenge is to use that knowledge to prevent what could be Earth's final disaster. The first step is to identify all possible doomsday rocks. Scientists use many tools, such as satellite images and spacecraft, to study asteroids and comets. They use these instruments, and scientific data gathered from past asteroid contact, to find out a doomsday rock's orbit.

When a possible doomsday rock is found, the next step is to determine when it will enter Earth's atmosphere. In July 1992, one asteroid was seen a dozen times. Scientists have a good idea of its orbit. Now they have to figure out its path around the sun. They will then know the asteroid's position for decades to come and will be able to predict whether or not it is a danger to Earth.

Is it possible to ward off a threatening space object? There are many ideas about how to save the earth from such an unwelcome visitor. Some involve the use of nuclear bombs; the people who like this idea hope that the bomb would blast the object and deflect it away from our planet. The problem is that a comet or an asteroid is millions of miles away. It is also moving extremely fast.

Iapetus, a moon of Saturn, has many craters shown in this image. Many of the planets and moons in our solar system have craters from collisions with asteroids and comets.

A doomsday rock would be approaching Earth at 67,000 miles (107,803 kilometers) per hour.

Problems

What if we actually could bomb the threatening object? The bombs that now exist could deflect a smaller space object, but for a large asteroid, the bomb might have to be ten thousand times more powerful than any that we have at this time. How would this weapon be delivered to the asteroid or the comet? An orbiting spacecraft loaded with such a cargo could be almost as dangerous as a killer rock from space would be.

There is another problem with bombing a doomsday rock. An atomic blast might shatter it into tiny pieces, or it might break it up into several large pieces instead. What if these pieces all plowed into Earth's surface? Our planet might survive, but there would be a lot of damage. Many lives would probably be lost.

It has been suggested that we do not actually have to bomb a doomsday rock. A nuclear bomb could be detonated miles away from the object. The radiation from the explosion would vaporize material from the surface of the asteroid, nudging it in the opposite direction. This would change the doomsday rock's velocity, altering its threatening course. Over millions of miles, that short distance would be magnified. Earth would be saved.

A comet's course could also be changed if it were hit with a huge heating device. The quickly melting ice would cause more jets of steam. Those jets might steer the comet away from Earth or slow it down. But they also might speed up the comet's journey *toward* our planet.

Some people are concerned that the storage and use of super-bombs would be almost as dangerous as a killer rock from space. They are worried that one of them might be set off accidentally or would explode too soon. They say that the radiation from a nuclear explosion in space may put our planet in peril.

Probes, such as the one shown in this illustration, may be deployed if an asteroid is spotted traveling on a trajectory toward Earth.

Scientists reply that there would be no more danger from superbombs than from the nuclear weapons that already exist. All such weapons are surrounded by security and have built-in safeguards to prevent any accidents. Their direction and time of detonation can be precisely controlled. A weapon directed at a doomsday rock would be detonated millions of miles from Earth. At that distance, the radiation would do us no harm.

Still, the use of nuclear weapons is enough of a worry to cause some experts to search for other methods of dealing with killer rocks from space. They suggest that a solar sail could deflect a dangerous comet. This device would catch the charged particles that stream from the sun and affect a comet's orbit. Their capture by the sail would cause the comet's path to be changed.

An orbiting mirror could focus a tight beam of sunlight on a threatening asteroid. The ray would vaporize part of the asteroid's surface. A jet of dust and ash would be created. Over months or years, that jet could shove the asteroid away from Earth. Another idea would be to use the space shuttle to place a shield in orbit around our planet.

Of course, all of these ideas have problems. Currently, one of the best methods scientists have come up with is called the gravitational tractor. This theory suggests sending a spacecraft to hover near the asteroid. The spacecraft's thrusters would angle outward from the asteroid, so they would not touch the surface.[4] The gravitational pull of the thrusters would change the asteroid's path just enough over a long period of time to direct it away from Earth.

Another theory suggests using antimatter to deflect the killer rock.[5] All mass is composed of very small particles of matter. Each of these particles has a corresponding particle of antimatter. When matter meets antimatter, they both self-destruct in a *poof* of pure energy. No one knows how the antimatter could be delivered to the space object, though. Because a rocket is made of matter, it would be destroyed as soon as the antimatter cargo was loaded.

An asteroid being pulled by a solar sail. It is believed that light from the sun would exert tiny amounts of pressure on the sail, which would enable it to accelerate and change the direction of an Earth-bound object.

The PS1 telescope in Hawaii is used to find and track asteroids, comets, and other near-Earth objects. Several observatories around the world are dedicated to this task.

Playing the odds

There is no shortage of ideas about how to deal with a killer rock from space. All of them would be very expensive. We have limited amounts of money and resources.

During one human lifetime, there is about a one in twenty thousand chance that a mountain-sized rock will crash into Earth. During that same lifetime, a person may be killed in a car crash or be infected with a fatal disease. An 8.0 earthquake could destroy an entire city. Should we spend our money to improve driver safety, find a cure for the disease, or to find a way to predict earthquakes? Or should we spend it to outwit a killer rock from space?

Dangerous asteroids and comets are out there. Someday, one of them will be on a collision course with Earth. Perhaps for now we should just watch the skies. There are scientists around the world who study near-Earth objects (NEOs).

A remnant linked to the 2008 TC3 asteroid found in the Nubian Desert in Sudan.

These people are part of Spaceguard associations or foundations that exist independently in many countries to help support the study of near-Earth objects. Spaceguard scientists could discover a doomsday rock early enough to prepare a defense.

In fact, on October 6, 2008, scientists using a telescope at the Catalina Sky Survey in Arizona detected the 2008 TC3 asteroid. After the small asteroid was discovered, a few other space observatories around the world followed its path and recorded data. The TC3 asteroid exploded in Earth's atmosphere the next day. Scientists were able to accurately predict the impact time and location. This was a historic moment, as it was the first time in history that an object had been observed before it was to hit Earth.

Despite the advances in observing doomsday rocks, human beings may yet meet the same fate as that of the dinosaurs. But we may not. We are the only species that is aware of the danger. We are the only species that would be able to do something about it.

The Greatest Show in Outer Space

The comet was formed as our solar system was being formed. For 4.5 billion years, it traced a path through outer space. Then the sun nudged it off its usual course. Fifty years ago, it was caught in the pull of Jupiter's gravity. Each time it orbited the planet, it was drawn deeper into the Jovian atmosphere. In 1992, the force of the planet's gravity started ripping apart the icy dust ball. The glowing string of fragments continued to orbit Jupiter.

In March 1994, astronomers Carolyn and Eugene Shoemaker and David Levy spotted a long, fuzzy-looking object in outer space. They identified the object as a comet, and it became known as Comet Shoemaker-Levy 9. At the time of discovery, Shoemaker-Levy 9 consisted of at least twenty-one large pieces and thousands of smaller ones. They were approaching the far side of Jupiter, the side that always faces away from Earth. All the larger pieces were on a collision course with the planet. It was predicted that the first fragment would plunge into Jupiter's gaseous surface on July 16, 1994.

Jupiter is two and a half times more massive than all the other planets combined. More than thirteen hundred Earths could be

This computer artwork shows a fragment of Comet Shoemaker-Levy 9 approaching Jupiter (right). Debris forming the tail of the comet trails behind it. Large pieces of the comet crashed into the far side of Jupiter in July 1994.

packed inside it. Astronomers believed that the large body could easily survive the blows of the comet fragments.

They did not know what either the immediate or the long-term effects of the pummeling would be. By the spring of 1994, hundreds of telescopes on Earth were focused on the shattered comet. Cameras on board two spacecraft were set to take pictures of the collision.

Pummeling Jupiter

On Saturday, July 16—right on schedule—the first fragment crashed onto Jupiter. The mountain-sized clump created a fireball half the size of Earth. The bubble of superheated gas was brighter than anything else on Jupiter. It was brighter than Io, its brightest moon.

By Sunday evening, seven fragments had blasted through the planet's whirling cloud cover. They were traveling at more than 130,000 miles (209,170 kilometers) per hour, sixty times faster than the speed of a bullet. The rock-hard chunks of ice and dust had built up a tremendous energy of motion. When they hit Jupiter's wispy cloud cover, friction stopped them dead.

The smallest of the larger pieces was only a half-mile wide, but it exploded with the force of 10 million megatons of TNT. It left a spreading plume of hot gas and debris as large as Earth. Such a collision would vaporize the city of Los Angeles in an instant. It would be the worst natural disaster ever experienced by human beings.

Each impact produced a mammoth fireball. The temperature at their centers was at least 53,000°F (29,000°C). The impacts left huge black scars on the far side of Jupiter. The heat was so intense that the atmosphere was speckled with many pieces of fried debris. Fiery plumes shot up hundreds of miles. The flames edged over Jupiter's horizon, where they became visible to telescopes on Earth.

On Monday morning, a two-mile-wide (three-kilometer-wide) fragment streaked sixty miles (ninety-seven kilometers) into Jupiter's atmosphere. Its blast was hundreds of times more powerful than the combined energy of all of our planet's nuclear weapons. The fireball it created spewed 1,300 miles (2,092 kilometers) into space. It was fifty times more luminous than Jupiter—so bright that, for a moment, it blinded the largest telescopes on Earth.

A panoramic view from a telescope of Shoemaker-Levy 9.

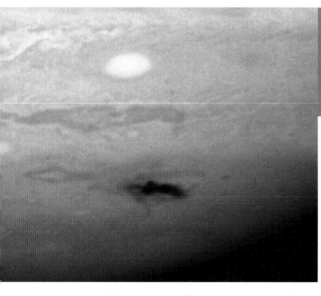

The Hubble Space Telescope captured this photo of Jupiter on July 23, 2009.

That collision gave Jupiter a "black eye" 9,600 miles (15,446 kilometers) across. The impact site was twice as large as Earth.

Two more fragments struck on Tuesday. The white-hot glow created by one of them was three times the size of Earth. By now, raging storms were ripping through Jupiter's atmosphere. On Wednesday, five more pieces of the dying comet added to the turbulence. They stirred up the brimstone soup of sulfur, ammonia, hydrogen, and helium. As David Levy remarked, "Jupiter has had the stuffing knocked out of it."[1]

Thursday saw the explosions of four mountain-sized fragments. They created overlapping fireballs at ten-hour intervals. The blackened impact sites were so close that they almost merged into each other.

The final large fragment struck after midnight, July 22, adding its plume to the ring of swirling, superheated gas. The comet was now completely destroyed, and, as predicted, the planet Jupiter had survived the battering.[2]

The spectacular cosmic show lasted only days, but what we learn from Shoemaker-Levy 9 will last forever. "The best way to find out about something is to poke it and see what happens," one astronomer said. "We just gave the atmosphere of Jupiter a giant poke."

A Chance to Learn

Most scientists used to believe that Earth had been formed by a series of gradual changes. Then they saw the neatly arranged rows of craters on two of Jupiter's moons, and the random scattering of craters on our own moon. Now, for the first time, human beings had seen how these craters were formed. It was clear that the bodies in our solar system were shaped largely by stupendous explosions.

What we can learn from Shoemaker-Levy 9 goes far beyond Jupiter itself. Perhaps we will get a better idea of how comets formed our own planet, how comets brought water to Earth, or how they brought life to Earth. The knowledge that we gain will help us better understand our entire solar system. It could give us the key to unlock some of the secrets of the universe.

CHAPTER NOTES

Chapter 1. The Reign of the Dinosaur

1. Lawrence Pringle, *Dinosaurs and Their World* (New York: Harcourt Brace, 1968), p. 38.
2. William Stout, *The Dinosaurs* (New York: Bantam Books, 1981), p. 4.
3. Carl Zimmer, "The Smoking Crater," *Discover*, January 1992, p. 48.

Chapter 2. The Search for Clues

1. Nigel Calder, *The Comet is Coming* (New York: Penguin Books, 1980), p. 124.
2. Ibid., p. 125.
3. Carl Zimmer, "The Smoking Crater," *Discover*, January 1992, p. 46.

Chapter 3. Life in the Fast Lane

1. David H. Levy, *The Quest for Comets* (New York: Plenum Press, 1994), p. 7.

Chapter 4. Outwitting a Doomsday Rock

1. David H. Levy, *The Quest for Comets* (New York: Plenum Press, 1994), pp. 10–11.
2. Ibid., p. 216.
3. Ibid.
4. Edward T. Lu and Stanley G. Love, "Gravitational tractor for towing asteroids," *Nature.com*, November 9, 2005, <http://www.nature.com/nature/journal/v438/n7065/abs/438177a.html> (December 10, 2009).
5. "Vision for the 21st Century," *Ad Astra*, June 1990, pp. 26–29.

Chapter 5. The Greatest Show in Outer Space

1. Sharon Begley and Mary Hager, "Good Show, by Jove," *Newsweek*, August 1, 1994, p. 60.
2. Ibid., p. 62.

GLOSSARY

asteroid—A small planetlike object in space.

astronomer—A person who studies objects and matter outside the earth's atmosphere, and what physical and chemical properties make up those objects.

atmosphere—The mass of air surrounding Earth.

carnivore—An animal that eats meat.

comet—A space object made of ice, gases, and dust that orbits the sun.

extinct—No longer existing.

fossil—Any trace of an extinct plant or animal that has been preserved in the earth's crust.

geology—The science and study of the history of Earth and its life that is found in rocks.

gravitational pull—The attraction that one object has for another due to the force of gravity.

herbivore—An animal that eats only plants.

iridium—A metal found in meteorites.

Jovian—Having to do with the planet Jupiter.

megaton—A million tons.

meteor—A rock, iron, or icy object that enters Earth's atmosphere.

meteorite—A stone or metallic meteor that has fallen to Earth's surface from space.

near-Earth object (NEO)—An object in the solar system whose orbit brings it into close proximity with Earth.

orbit—A path of one body in its rotation about another (as in the earth around the sun).

radiation—The process of giving off radiant energy, or heat, in the form of waves or particles.

tektite—A glassy rounded object formed in the sudden heat and release of gases.

vaporize—To convert, or become gas.

FURTHER READING

Books

Kusky, Timothy. *Asteroids and Meteorites: Catastrophic Collisions With Earth.*
New York: Facts on File, 2009.

Miller, Ron. *Asteroids, Comets, and Meteors.* Minneapolis, Minn.: Twenty-First
Century Books, 2006.

Mist, Rosalind. *Could an Asteroid Hit the Earth?: Asteroids, Comets, Meteors,
and More.* Chicago: Heinemann Library, 2006.

Nardo, Don. *Asteroids and Comets.* Greensboro, N.C.: Morgan Reynolds Pub.,
2009.

Parks, Peggy J. *Killer Asteroids.* Farmington Hills, Mich.: KidHaven Press,
2006.

Sherman, Josepha. *Asteroids, Meteors, and Comets.*
New York: Marshall Cavendish Benchmark, 2010.

Internet Addresses

Asteroid Introduction
<http://www.solarviews.com/eng/asteroid.htm>

NASA—Comets
<http://www.nasa.gov/worldbook/comet_worldbook.html>

INDEX